[handwritten inscription]

Odysseus' Homecoming
&
The New Adam
Poems of Renewal

[handwritten signature] Bahman Sho... 9/9/11

Books by Bahman Sholevar
Available in English

Making Connection: Poems of Exile
The Angel with Bush-Baby Eyes *and Other Poems*
The Love Song of Achilles *and Other Poems*
Odysseus' Homecoming (Poem)
The New Adam: Poems of Renewal
Night's Journey (Novel)
The Creative Process: A Psychoanalytic Discussion
  (with William G. Niederland)

Odysseus' Homecoming
&
The New Adam
Poems of Renewal

Bahman Sholevar

Concourse  Press

Box 28600 Overbrook Station
Philadelphia, Pennsylvania 19151

Manufactured in the United States of America
First edition, 1982
Cover design by Patricia Randels
Library of Congress Catalog Card Number 82-73948
ISBN 0-911323-05-8

For my brother, Javad

Table of Contents

Odysseus' Homecoming 1
  Odysseus' Homecoming 3

The New Adam 39
  The New Eve 41
  Song of Diogenes 43
  New Adam to Maximus of Gloucester 51

Odysseus' Homecoming

Odysseus' Homecoming

Odysseus, the steadfast man,
versatile, deliberate,
man of destiny, man of woe,
master of battle and of war,
has fulfilled Teiresias'
sooth and the will of
Zeus, the grim King,
and has now come home,
home to stony Ithaca,
alone, friendless.

Alone he has survived
the headlong death,
the western gloom,
and the unnumbered dead.
Alone he has endured
the long war and
the lordly water, fought
the blue-maned god of the sea,
to save his own life and bring
his shipmates home, alive.

Alone he has crossed
the Western Ocean on a raft,
his metal proven seaworthy,
Odysseus, the great wanderer,
master mariner and soldier,
adventurer and king,
has now come home where
he ate bread in childhood,
and took joy of life.

Alone surviving
the nymph's flesh,
the sorceress' magic,
and the siren's song,
now he has made shore,
in the twentieth year,
come to home and wife,
he who had long hungered for both,
now weary with old age,
looking forth to that
soft seaborne death,
promised him by Zeus
through Teiresias'
bloodthirsty sooth.

Having brought bawdy death
in one bloody swoop
to the beefeating suitors,
and the fun-loving maids,
with a little help from
his friend, Zeus's virgin child,
the grey-eyed goddess,
now he stands upon
his fields of home, upon the
threshold of his timbered hall,
Odysseus, master of disguises,
master of the tall tale,
now shedding the disguise
and the tale, bared
to his naked flesh and
the wild boar's wound,
stands godlike against
the pillar of the well-wrought
roof, stands before

the mistress of the household,
Penelope of the milkwhite arms,
weaving at the master loom.

But there is no astonishment
in that Queen's face, nor joy,
nothing but sorrowful content
at the indifferent task
of weaving a death shroud
for his long-gone Lord's father.
He looks on and she weaves,
not looking up from her loom
at the beggar now trans-
formed into a king,
she who has not had the use too long
of either a beggar or a king,
she who has lacked
so much so long
the very taste buds have
faded from her memory.
Who is that man, she asks.
Is it thanks he wants
for the killing of my suitors?
Or is it some other bounty?
The answer fails her.
Everyone knows him but her,
everyone takes joy of him,
for he has things to give,
to everyone but her.
To the swineherd,
he will give swine,
to the cowherd, cows, tenfold,
and fine shirts and cloaks,
and lances to keep dogs at bay;

and to them he will give houses,
and young women to wed.
The old nurse will have her joy
of the infant Odysseus
and his telltale boar's wound.
She will have bracelets
and anklets of hammered gold,
and embroidered slippers,
and the price of twenty oxen
Laertes had paid for her purchase.
Telemachus will have his
patrimony, and a king for a father,
a strong Odysseus to defend him.
But what is he bringing her?
Her lost carriage and comeliness,
her faded beauty and youth,
all gone because of
Helen's easy virture?

And there Odysseus stands,
master of many crafts,
master of stratagems,
master of subtle ways
and straight, the wily master
of sea ways and of land ways,
master of the spoken word,
for once the words failing him,
for once without speech, before
this silent majestic queen,
weaving at her loom,
who will not be awed
by his manly warrior's flesh,
nor by his wild boar's wound,
nor by his shock of arms,

nor his skill in the art of death.
There he stands on his own
threshold, the lord of the tall house,
the patient hero, steady, quiet,
yet wounded in his deep heart,
waiting to be acknowledged,
beggar or king, waiting
to be reckoned with.
And at last he speaks:

"Mistress and Queen!
It is I, Odysseus,
the look and bulk of him,
not a beggar, who stands
before your knees,
demanding recognition,
demanding justice.
No way in this world is
Odysseus dead, nor another
Odysseus will ever come,
for he and I are one,
the girlhood husband
you have so long lacked.
Twenty years I have fought
dark headlong death.
Long have I cleaved my way
through the wars of men.
The winedark sea has had
its will with me long.
This is a cold homecoming,
indeed, for a brave king,
for a man who has long
hungered for wife and home,
who has breasted the broadback sea

and challenged the willful gods,
to see once more the hearthsmoke
leaping upward from his roof.
Indeed, the immortal gods
must have made you hard,
put an iron heart in your breast,
to stand thus aloof from
your lord and king, come home
to you in the twentieth year."

And the Mistress and Queen
replies, majestic and cold:

"That you are Odysseus,
my girlhood husband and my king,
whom I have long bitterly needed,
I know and I grant.
But demand nothing more of me,
who have nothing more to give.
What your will is demand,
not from me but from
the easeful gods,
whose favorite you are,
and who can give what
your heart may desire."

And Odysseus, the kingly man,
smiled a self-endearing smile,
content for now to have been recognized:

"Mistress! Gods have given
their share. They delivered to me
and to the flowing-haired Achaeans,
in the tenth year of our siege,

Priam's city and proud Ilion's
citadel, for which I will burn many
a fat thighbone on Zeus's altar.
And this day they have delivered
into my hands the swinish suitors
who had wished to sleep in my soft bed,
and whom I have killed in triumph,
for which a hecatomb is due
Athena and the immortal gods.
Now I await what only a woman
can give, and no god."

And the Queen makes
indifferent answer:

"Odysseus! It is justice you want.
And justice you will have,
none from my hand,
nor from my heart.
A queen's justice is not
a king's, to love one at will,
and abhor another at whim.
Ask not for my thanks for
the killing of my suitors
and the slaughter of my maids.
For four years now, had those
suitors been my only joy,
waiting upon my runaway youth,
attending my every favor,
mirroring in their glad eyes
my fading beauty. I did not
dishonor your marriage bed of oak.
They had not their wish of me.

But I had my modest joy
in their carefree faces,
and in their boisterous ways.
I who lacked Clytaemnestra's gumption
and Helen's gall, nevertheless,
had my desires in my fancy.
Night after night I mused on
their gleaming looks, caressed
in fancy each scarce-bearded face.
And gods in their mercy sent
pleasant dreams through ivory gates,
to warm my pure cold sheets.
Those suitors you killed, Odysseus,
they were the fat geese of my dreams.
Demand no thanks from me
for the killing of my geese."

And Odysseus, the patient hero,
the noble and enduring man,
whom they compared even to the gods,
stood cold as a stone,
yet felt the burning of
the blood in his iron veins.
Must he drink wormwood and bear
insult under his own roof?
His words when he spoke were
calm and cold, yet they were
the words of a sceptered king,
one whose wrath one may well heed:

"Queen! These are bold words
to speak to one's Lord and King.

You would be well advised to be wary.
It is impiety to gloat over the dead,
but would you mourn the rutting suitors,
fat on my meat, and their harlots,
to the gall of your own lord?
Or is it that you and the gods
are still testing my forbearance?
Must Laertes' son be once more offended?
Have I not had enough,
what with the Cyclops' fury
and Poseidon's willful ways?
For ten years I suffered
on Troy's wide seaboard,
and for ten more I wandered,
over the winedark sea, beating
my way home, while Poseidon
spun dark days for me.
Have I survived the suitors' deadly
broadswords and keen spears
to this here cold homecoming
and a wife's brazen words?"

And the queen of the milkwhite arms,
the dear cunning Penelope,
not even looking up from the loom,
still weaving, replied:

"What will you do, Odysseus?
Will you kill me, too?
Will you burn out my eyes?
You have had your reward
more than I, or any mortal
can give. You alone, of all men
have tasted the nymph's cool flesh

11

and the sorceress' lust, lying
in Circe's flawless bed of love,
in an island, in the running sea.
You alone, of all mortals,
have heard the sirens' song,
and have lived to tell.
You have had your will
with the proud height of Troy,
have sacked Ilion's holy shrine,
have lorded it over King
Priam's fallen city, lying with
many a conquered king's daughter.
Was Nausicaa of sunbright hair
kind to you on that riverbank,
before she led you on
to her father's guilded hall?

Odysseus, you have fulfilled
your destiny and Zeus's will,
going to war to Ilion
on an ill wind.
But what was my destiny?
Weaving away my life,
my beauty and my youth,
until dark death came for me?
Many a night I sat alone,
under the full moon,
by the halfmoon bay,
cursing Helen's beauty
and my own youth,
shedding salt tears
into the salt sea.
Twenty years is a dog's
lifetime and the fading time

for the beauty of a young
woman in mint condition.
Helen has her beauty yet,
and her youth, Helen
for whose dubious virtue
many a son's mother
and a mother's son died.
Was every burnt mother and infant
in Troy guilty for Helen's
wantonness and for Paris's lust?
But Helen is half a goddess,
if half an adulteress.
She will live forever,
will be forever young,
the bastard daughter of Zeus.
Gods look after their own.
They stand up for adulterers.
Woe for Queen Clytaemnestra, who
for her adultery so dearly paid."

And King Odysseus,
Laertes' royal son,
now spoke full with
righteous indignation:

"Woman! Dare you defend an adulteress,
and a king-killer to boot, who
with her two-faced pander of a man
drove her lord and king in ignoble death,
to the sunless world, felling him
like an ox feeding at the trough?
Nor would she close his eyes,
nor close his mouth, nor would pay
Charon the dread ferryman, his fare

to ferry the soul over the marsh
of flowing sorrows."
And Penelope, Icarius' daughter,
queen of sad eyes, and of
sad voice, replied:

"She gave a daughter in sacrifice,
to buy an ill wind for a proud king,
that he may bring home an adulteress,
and bring home conquered king's daughters,
to lie with him in his soft bed.
And did not King Agamemnon
for the sake of one glancing-eyed girl
dishonor god Apollo and drive to distraction
Peleus' son, that Hector may triumph
over so many dead Achaeans and drive
their souls like dead leaves
to the house of Death?
And did he not dishonor his own
marriage vows, preferring her
to his own wedded wife?
But what have I to do
with that ill-fated queen?
No, I gave no daughter
for that ill wind, no daughter
of my womb, to buy back
Helen of Argos for her Lord,
only twenty years of my life,
a small price for a big venture.
And if my marriage vows
were defiled by my Lord
and my King, it was at least
not with mortal flesh, but with
goddesses, nymphs, and sorcerers."

And Lord Odysseus,
the deep-lunged man
of battle, now raging:

"Now the weird is upon me!
Woman, dare you question the will
of Zeus and the immortal gods on high?"

And Penelope,
the deep-minded queen,
soft-spoken, now replied:

"Odysseus, gods often bid
men's fancy's bidding.
And you, alas, have been
too willing to obey.
The gods that have appeared to you
have been the messengers
of your own desires.
Gods know well how
to delude a willing man."

And Odysseus, light of councils:

"Nay! What I have done was
for no want of prophecy.
Zeus himself sent me
through his own royal bird,
and men keen at reading birdflight,
many an indisputable bird sign."

And Penelope, the witty queen:

"Odysseus! Bird signs are
for birds, not for men.
Was it the will of Zeus
or your greed and prurience
that led you to the Cyclops' cave,
for which your men perished?
Was it a god who commanded you
to blind Lord Poseidon's son,
to delay your homecoming,
and add to my lonely
years by half a score?
And did you not all but lose
your ship and your men
to your wanton Noman's bragging?
Must my beauty and youth pay
for your shipmates' unruliness,
wasting Lord Helios' peaceful kine,
Lord of the high noon,
while you took a midday nap?
Well they paid for it in salt blood,
but you were the brilliant one.
You were the grey-eyed Athena's
fair-haired boy, the one
who always got away.
You always had a patroness,
a goddess, a sorceress, a nymph.
And while your men were wasted
by the orb-eyed Cyclops and by Scylla,
the monster of the grey rock,
your fame grew all over
Hellas and midland Argos.
And your destiny was fulfilled.

Your tale will be told in song
for many a generation to come.
As for me, I had no destiny.
I had to make myself a name,
the only way I knew how,
by kindling the fire of desire
in men whom I cared not to satisfy,
by weaving and unweaving
a death shroud amongst
the admiring lustful eyes
of the pride of Ithacan princes.
Yet though you would not grow
old, in Calypso's hollow caves,
where you enjoyed your cool nymph flesh,
my face and my eyes lost
their luster and their sheen,
by day and by night.
For twenty years I have had
a husband in name alone,
no husband of my bosom.
While you in your wayward ways
were nymphing and sorceressing,
these suitors were my only joy,
men to dress for, and shine upon.
A woman needs that. Twenty
years you have been gone,
twenty sad long years,
too long for loneliness,
too heavy for hope. Many
a night in my fancy's eye
I saw you standing in the door,
helmeted, lapped in gleaming bronze,
with a light hand on your spear,

graceful as a young god,
and my heart leaped with joy.
But it was a cruel hoax,
worked by cruel gods.
That was a mistake, Odysseus,
appearing to me in rags
after so many years,
making yourself look
older than you were.
There was your one chance
to rekindle my youthful fire,
and my one chance for illusion,
and you ruined them both.
I saw it all from the start,
saw through the rags,
and through your scheming mind,
plotting a dark hour
for the unmindful suitors.
And I had time enough, while
you plotted and you schemed,
to study your face, your
posture, and your ways.
And I observed and I compared.
I had married a young, handsome
prince, my girlhood husband,
had seen him off to a cruel war,
and now had kept a twenty-year-old vigil
for a broken old man's homecoming,
who had appeared to me in rags,
still lusting for hot blood.
The terror I had suffered,
the cruel long years, first
wishing each day for your return,

but fearing the news of your death;
then not knowing whether
you were dead, your body lying
on the dark earth at the sea's edge,
unmourned, unburied, fed by dogs
and carrion birds, your bones rotting
white in the rain, or tumbling
in the groundswell of the sea;
then not caring, tired of
not knowing, then wishing
you were dead, and wishing
to know you were dead, that I
may have a new beginning.
A woman's beauty and flesh,
unlike an old soldier's skill,
do not improve with time.
A woman has her season
and she must be consumed
before she is too ripe."

The knees gave under Odysseus,
the old soldier, breaker of men,
who had wrung manhood from
the knees of many; who amongst
all the Achaean host
that made war on Troy,
had not a rival
for steadiness
and a stout heart.
His heart sickened.
Now cried out in pain,
the great-lunged man of battle:

"Lord Poseidon,
dread god of the sea!
Your might extends thus far,
even to this highmark
of stony Ithaca, to revenge
your son's blinded eye, and spoil
and old soldier's homecoming.
Has ten years of spinning
dark days for me
on the winedark sea
not been enough to pay
ransom for a giant's eye?

Giving twenty years of my life
to fulfill the will of Zeus,
must I now come home
to a wife's ingratitude
under my own roof?"

And Queen Penelope,
queen of ivory arms,
queen of the busy loom, replied:

"Odysseus, what gods denied,
denied us both, life together
in our prime and full flower,
passing gracefully into age.
You have come home looking forth
to a mild death drifting
upon you from the sea.
You have had your youth
and now will have your age.
I have had neither youth,

nor am ready for graceful age.
The joyless years you
and the gods spun for me,
have indeed been dark.
Helen of Argos lay
half a score of years
in a seducer's bed,
and in her husband's
the other half,
and she has her renown
and her inhuman beauty still.
She walks straight as a shaft
of gold, gracing the halls of
her dishonored Lord, the red-haired
King Menelaus of the great war cry.
But what have I, the faithful wife,
whose beauty has stood the siege
of two scores of lords and princes,
and even more cruel, of
twenty desolate years?"

And Odysseus,
the raider of cities,
the brave conquerer of Troy,
the great improviser, now spoke:

"But we have each other now.
I am the same Odysseus who left
for Ilion in a hollow ship.
I can still string my mighty
bow and whip an arrow through
twelve axe heads, shooting
straight to thread the iron."

And Penelope, the wise queen:

"Aye, Odysseus! But I am not
the same Penelope who was left
behind by those same hollow ships.
I have lost gift of joy, and
have lost gift of laughter,
and have lost gift of sleep.
My blood has turned sickly cold,
my flesh has lost its bounce.
Will you have me go hot to bed
after twenty years of cold sheets?
Will you quicken in one night
twenty dead years of loss?
I lack the sorcerer's magic
and the nymph's knack.
The easeful gods who live forever,
can have their eternal sport,
but men live and die in time;
in time women's beauty withers,
their hopes grow faint and die,
their skin turn sickly with waiting.
Will the immortal gods give me back
my faded beauty and youth?
Odysseus, the war the gods won
for you, Troy alone did not lose.
I, too, lost that war. I alone
came off with no prizes.
Aphrodite had her golden apple,
and Ox-eyed Lady Hera her revenge,
and Athena, the beautiful one,
the perfect one, had hers too,
sporting with my queenly life.
Now let Poseidon rule

the winedark sea, and
Zeus, the rainmaker have
his laughter in the clouds,
but mind me, now!
I will have my way!
Zeus will not have
his way with me, nor
Athena her gamesmanship!"

And Odysseus, the pious one,
who ever made libations to
the gods, and burned
thighbones of goats and cows
laid in fat, on their altars,
now replied:

"Queen and Lady!
These are wicked words to hurl
at mighty gods. Let Zeus be not
angry at us for this impiety!
Beware the wrath of Heaven's
dread king, lest he might wield
his lightning and strike!
Will you dare to match wit
and evasion with immortal gods?
But if gods must be left out
of our affair, so be it!
If you will not have me a king,
let me claim a husband's right,
and that of my son's father.
And if that should not move you,
let me be a beggar again, and
beggar to queen, let me
touch your knees, and

be a suppliant on mine."

And Penelope,
the sad-eyed queen, heavyhearted,
now ceased at her loom:

"No, Odysseus!
Do not kneel! There is
no crossing this river now.
There lies too much blood between
us, too much estrangement,
too much nymph's flesh,
too much adultery,
though not mine.
Iphigenia's blood cries out
from the altar, a daughter
sacrificed by a father's hand;
and Queen Clytaemnestra's blood,
shed by a god-ridden son, and
the blood of every mother
and of every son shed in
King Priam's burning city,
and the blood of all those
Achaean gentlemen with flowing hair,
who died on Troy's wide seaboard,
and the blood of my green suitors,
and the blood of my pink maids.
And King Agamemnon's tall shade
will nightly leave the sunless
house of Death, to lie abed
between man and wife, and
chill the hot blood of desire.
This much justice, Odysseus,
you will have from me,

and this much truth.
Though no husband-killer I,
yet I did admire that deadly queen's
courage and magnificent revenge,
and did mourn her woeful death,
forged by a son's hand."

And Odysseus, the guileful master,
cool-headed, quick, fair-spoken,
now replied with craft and gall,
still looking for a stratagem,
to storm this willful queen's citadel:

"But what will you do, Queen?
You have no more suitors to marry.
They are all quite dead,
soft men who had fancied,
to bed in a lion's den."

And you replied, Penelope —
O my magnificent queen —:

"Odysseus, now it is time
for you to learn that to lie
with in soft beds, women prefer
soft men. A warrior is good
at war, not in love.
And an old warrior is
so much the worse in both.
Let warriors lie with slave
girls, the prizes they have won.

And what will you do, King?
You who have lost your queen
to time, and your slave girls
to the pirate sea."

And Lord Odysseus, the brave
king, of the seed of Zeus, feeling
the fit coming upon him again,
now raged with dark anger:

"Woman, now you try my patience!
Beware an old man's rage!
The killing of your suitors
has not quite blunted my sword.
There is still some frolic left
in the old knife. Goad me
to the edge, and be you
ten times my son's mother,
it will not save you.
By Heavens! I have killed many
a son's mother in my days!"

And now Penelope,
the deep-minded queen,
looked up from her loom,
and faced the man she spoke to:

"I know! That too, Odysseus,
has been on my mind. And
to little wonder, now that
even sons murder their mothers.
Who will decide which adulteress
shall live, and which shall die?
Helen still lives, whose inhuman

birth, when Zeus had his joy of
Leda, brought dark forebodings
for the days of my youth.
And Artemis, pure Artemis,
spares her still her shafts."

And now Odysseus was silent.
No treasure he had brought
from the long war and wandering,
could make up for his losses at home.
Neither cunning, nor craft, nor love,
could move this restive queen.
And there was no fear in her,
neither of man nor of gods. He
made one more desperate charge:

"But right or wrong, queen,
I have honored you, and
I have loved you."

And to this, O my queen, you replied:

"Odysseus, you have loved
the sea ways dearer than
you have loved wife and home.
And you have loved war
dearer than you have loved me.
You have loved plunder and
carnage better than plowing
a terraced land. Nothing you
can offer, will move me now.
I have waited this long
to make my peace with
you, before I go."

And King Odysseus, light of councils,
wide-eyed and wide-mouthed,
now said:

"But where will you go,
obstinate, wretched queen?
Back to your lordly father's
home, without treasures,
without queenly honors?"

And to this, Penelope,
the attentive queen, replied:

"No, it is not to my father's
home, I wish to return. Where
I am bound, I shall not need
treasures nor queenly honors."

And Odysseus now thought
of King Agamemnon's admonition
on the sunless fields of asphodel,
that the day of faithful wives
was gone forever. He asked:

"Have you another suitor, Queen?"

And Penelope of ivory skin,
looking her lord boldly in the face:

"Aye!"

And Odysseus, the lost man,
feeling a sting deep in his marrow,
yet keeping his cool, pursued:

"A prince?"

And Penelope the iron queen replied:

"No, I have had enough
of kings and princes,
of captains and warlords,
of gods and mortal sons of gods.
No more princes for me!
No more men of destiny,
beloved or hated of the gods!
Give me a plain simple man,
a man I can call mine,
and never fear to lose.
Penelope is now for merriment,
to squeeze out some simple joy
from her remaining days."

And now King Odysseus rose,
looking godlike and erect,
with awesome terror in his face.
His words came cold and steady:

"King to Queen, one thing
I must know, Lady!
Has any soft man slept
in my iron bed and lain
beside my queenly wife?"

And to this you replied,
Penelope — O my playful queen—:

"Why, will you kill him too?
Have you not had enough of killing?

Can there be no quittance
for you but by death?
Must you ever speak to men
through votive blood?
If you kill him, kill me too!
And give us both a tomb together,
as merciful Orestes did with
his mother and her soft man."

And now godlike Odysseus,
Laertes' royal son,
of the seed of Zeus,
took a mighty oath:

"I swear by the nine rings
of the river Styx, and by the eternal
marsh of flowing sorrow, an oath
that even gods cannot forswear,
that I will not touch him,
should there be such a man,
nor will I spill your blood.
But, Queen, I must know!"

And you replied, O my queen:

"Then put some heart into you,
Odysseus, and nerve yourself!
For I will tell you! Then
we shall see, whether you
who could stand your ground
in war, can now stand your ground
in peace, with no more killing.
Killing is a wartime business,

and odious even at that. Of
the twenty years you were gone,
I spent ten years in tears,
while you gave battle on
Troy's wide seaboard. Then
came news of the city's fall,
and I waited for three years
in joy and in hope for my
triumphant lord's return.
Three more years I spent in fear,
while you made your passage home.
Warrior after warrior returned,
lord after lord, but my own
true Lord and King never came.
I listened to many a wandering sailor,
from many a wayward ship, gave my ear
to any man who had a tale to tell, for
a free meal and a spread of sheepskin.
And I heard many a tall tale.
One man had you tied down to Egypt
on a windless sea; another in thralldom
to the nymph Calypso, in her cool caves;
a third man put you on Circe's island,
in the middle of the running sea, then
in Circe's flawless bed of love;
a fourth man saw you with the Cyclops,
in his bloody feast of men, then had you
free, boasting on the winedark sea, while
the blinded giant threw mountains at you;
a fifth swore you came to grief, and
perished with your men at sea, your bones
picked quite clean by some freeloading fish;

a sixth reported you in the house of Death,
hectoring it over marrowless shades of the dead.

At last I grew weary of the tales,
and closed my ears and my doors
to the yarns of men. I spent
the next three years in despair,
cursing Helen's beauty and my fate;
lost all joy in the affairs of men,
not caring whether I should live or die.

Nineteen years in all I gave you;
but this last year has been my own,
to give or do as I please,
since that fated day last summer,
when a strange ship put in at Argos harbor,
blown in by an indifferent wind,
and put a stranger ashore,
who came to my closed door a suppliant,
begging for a look at the queenly face
of King Odysseus' mythic wife. He
was a young man scarce bearded, scarce
older than my own true son, Telemachus,
blue of eyes and fair of hair, with
the radiance of a young god upon him,
with a look distant as a young god's.
Indeed, had I a mind to I could have
been persuaded that he was a god,
perhaps, Apollo of the silver bow, come
to save me from my wretched state,
or Zeus on one of his outings,
spinning dark days for another Troy.

But I went for the man,
who said he was no god,
nor mortal son of god,
nor prince, nor sea-faring
man, but a plain rustic
from sandy Pylos, a keeper
of vineyards, who plowed
a terraced plot, on a land
kind with grain, under
the wooded mountain.
And we let it go at that.
He stayed with me a night,
and we loved and he left.
But we swore a solemn oath,
that dead or alive, I would give
Odysseus another weary year, that
in a year's time my rustic would
return and take me, to his vineyard
under the wooded mountain. It is
he now who has my heart,
and I his, who swore has
known no other woman.
He is not much of a man.
No warrior he.
He will not pass
the test of the bow,
nor make the needle shot.
But for loneliness he will do.
He is a simple man, but
he is no coward, and no fool.
His laughter gives joy,
his love comfort and assurance.
With him I mean to
make a new beginning.

You have slaughtered
the suitors in vain."

And now King Odysseus,
light of councils,
master mind of war,
dreaded by men, and
beloved of the gods,
raised his hands in despair,
and called upon lordly Zeus:

"King of gods and of men! Lord
of high Heaven and dread thunder!
I have sworn a mighty oath
not to bring this man to book,
nor spill this woman's blood,
but you who rule the clouds
and wield the fearsome thunderbolt,
will you suffer that a sceptered
king, who has ever served your will,
be so basely abused. Oh that
I should lose my wife and my
queen to such a scapegrace,
a green rustic of a boy,
unbearded, a young buck
of a vineyard keeper!"

And Penelope of the milkwhite arms,
Icarius' daughter, now rose
tall, with the pride of
womanhood on her,
a moving grace,
and said:

"Spare the wrath of
your gods, my King!
You shall find they
have no power over
me and my rustic man.
Those who have nothing to
give, have nothing to fear.
If it is any comfort to you,
I will own this much:
You have lost me, not
to a better man, but
to a younger and humbler.
Women ask not for much
to be made happy."

And now King Odysseus'
brave heart broke.
And broke the spirit
in the greathearted man.
Down to his knees he went,
covered his face in his
mighty hands, and wept.
He in bitter grief had found
that what gods of heaven bid,
daughters of men do not approve.
Odysseus had been defeated
not by immortal gods,
nor by mortal sons
of men, but by time.

Long he sat thus, the defeated
king, and mused; long after
the light had gone under
the dark world's rim;

long after the Queen,
Penelope of the milkwhite
arms, had departed; long
after Prince Telemachus,
the King's own true son,
lay up indoors, daydreaming
of his great father, the
strong Odysseus he had
so bitterly needed so long.
And then the greathearted man
rememberd that his years of toil
were not yet at an end; that
the reckoning had not yet
been paid in full; that his
destiny was not yet fulfilled.
Lord Poseidon, the blue-maned god
of the sea, had yet to be appeased.
He recalled old seer Teiresias'
prophecy, and the immortal
gods' last bidding, that
he should take an oar, and
trudge the wide mainland,
until he reached a place
where men had never known
the dark blue sea, nor
sea-going ships, nor tasted
the flavor of salt meat,
until a passerby would say,
'Is that a winnowing fan on
your shoulder, strange sir?'
There he would plant the oar,
and make libation, and fair
sacrifice, to Lord Poseidon,
the god of the sea.

And with this, King Odysseus,
Lord of Penelope,
left his hall,
and his queen,
and his heartache,
and struck out alone,
again, to look for an oar.

The New Adam

Poems of Renewal

The New Eve

This diamondback
deadly
seductive
of easy grace
is not nuptial.
Her necessity
is not marriage
but love.
She will bed
but not wed.
If she says she
loves, she loves.
If it's otherwise
she'll say otherwise.
Broad-fronted, she wears
earrings of bastard emerald.
She has no sharp edges
smooth as mayonnaise.
Half queen, half commoner,
half mired and half admired,
she fears not
being blatant
nor being popular.
Being popular, she says,
is a whore's business.
No one went to heaven
just by being popular.
When she turns whore
she turns subtle whore.
Whether she comes
to you or you to her,

she always wins.
In a warm summer day
taking a break from tying
the loose ends of your life,
lounging on a beach
across from the Western Door,
you read Pablo Neruda and
fall in love with her.

Pablo, my boy,
this is your doing!
When she leaves,
this ocean perch,
you're all that's left
against the Western Door.

Song of Diogenes

I

Caught
all winter
made to choose
between something bad
and something worse
a public hell and
a private one
you chose privacy,
convinced
that suffering is
the only decent
thing left to do
the way out.

Sitting pretty
in your private hell
reading Plato on the
come-at-ability of souls
Plato wise Plato
(that geometry addict)
who forbade fish
condemned poets
and decreed
sharing of
wives,
cogitations
of a stale mind
of a winter's day.

All winter long
sitting pat on a bust
spouting profundities
reading Aquinas on grace
Pythagoras on beans,
ejaculations
of a spent mind
of a winter's day,
when the chill within
and the chill without
co-conspire to kill
a world already dead,
waiting for your
soul to arrive.
For the soul
always arrives
though not
by a shortcut.
There are no short-
cuts for the soul
no shortcuts bet-
ween the cabbage
town and the
primrose path.
The soul abides
its time, comes
the hard way
by the longest route
Others may not
know this,
others who have not
walked in your boots,
who know not
what devious route

a soul in agony
takes to arrive,
who know not
the desperate courage
that brings you
from there to here
against all odds,
may wonder to what
end all this hunger.

Full and forty
past your prime
past your middle
of the way, waiting
still waiting
for your soul
to be reborn
to be trans-
formed.
(Some say
there is no soul
before forty, not enough
silence there, not enough
space, only a penumbra
of distraction
of destruction
too much rush
of the blood.)

And when it comes
if you have been patient
if you have deserved your soul
what kind of soul
will it be?

Will it be a lion's soul
if a lion has a soul?
Or will it be a lamb's
if a lamb has a soul?
(In heaven where all souls go
will they say, there goes
the soul of a lion, there
the soul of a lamb?
Thus Pythagoras! Thus Plato!)

Will it be the two-fisted
soul of a meat-eater
ready to punch
through the world?
(I know, I have been
a bastard once or twice
in my own time, have
bruised a few gentle souls
have cracked a few skulls.
Slave to my pride
played the Heresiarch
of love and flesh,
was ambitious, vied
for the world's heart.
Once even competed
with the Bishop of Rome
for an audience
in Philadelphia
and lost to him big.
But I have always
minded the substance
and the forms of love.)

Will it be an old man's soul
on a yoghurt and hickory nut diet
doing spiritual bookkeeping?

Or will it be a poet's soul,
that magnificent bird,
rare, canary-colored,
full of strange songs?
For a soul like a bird
has its own progression,
through its forms of love,
transforming itself,
from a bird of prey
to a song bird, and then,
to a bird of paradise.
Then there is no more
taste of blood, no more
digging up of worms,
no more a diet of bugs.

The soul then feeds upon
the fragrance of roses
the aroma of faded songs
that fall like snowflakes
from the heaven of the mind.

The soul has its own
progression through the seasons.
The winter soul sits
cool-headed, patient,
feeling heavy with sleep,
feeling oppressed.
The spring soul is restless
has presentiments of

awakening of the blood
awakening of the trees
awakening of the birds.
It beats its head against
the bars of the cage.
The summer soul is careless.
It dances and sings and throws
all caution to the wind.
But the soul always wins
at the end, because
it knows how to wait.

II

What are these strange stirrings
with the first blush
of the spring?
Azalias blooming
magnolias blushing
forsythias taking to the field
dogwoods taking over
everything beyond itself
carried away, birds everywhere,
these daughters of song.
What are all these forebodings
of the fury of the summer?
Magnolias shedding tulips?
What's that dolphin doing
sitting out there on the grass?
To what end these cruel intimations
these vibrations in the
chilled bone of content?

The winter was more blissful
when love though dead,
was still here, when
the wind and the rain
had not shaken loose
last year's abandoned nest,
when faded melodies
were still playing
on the heart's
rusted harp
like the memory
of a friend, a lover,
though gone
still near at hand,
and yet as if years
and miles away;
though cold,
though cruel,
still a lover,
still a friend,
in the heart's bosom.
The taste of love
consummated, yet
not to the full,
a cup half drunk
yet not to the dregs,
leaving the heart
bitter and discontent.
Utter the magic word
the word of power
the word of love!
Magnolia!
Azalia!
Forsythia!

The word fails
because love has failed
because love has departed
from the scene.
The heart remains numb.

New Adam To Maximus of Gloucester

For Charles Olson

I

To you Maximus
of Gloucester
man-city
root-man
in root-city
this letter
post-haste from me
Maximus of Thin Air
man of no city
man of no roots
man with roots
hacked off
nothing but
my own headland
figure of inward
involuted
twisted
my tail i
ч   n
ʇnoɯ ʎɯ
feeding on
my own innards
chewing the cud
of my vegetable soul
not yet born or reborn
not yet consummated
or past consummation
the form of my love

without substance.
Here I stand
naked before you
not like a cherub before God
nor content as a worm.
Root-person without roots
here I stand
grounded
islanded
outside my elements
bare isolated exposed
yet none the more revealed.
I have come
across rough waters
in search of coherence
seeking out
a polis any polis
that will cover
my nakedness.
Yours will do
it will have to.
Yes, meet me anywhere
anywhere at all
anywhere there are
no billboards
someone selling
their mothers
free for ten days
satisfaction guaranteed
or just pay the return postage.
And the place need not have
a fancy name either
it could even be
where there are

little magazines,
no, not to publish me
I am published out
not to barter neither
my your our trade
I know poetry is
a living business
nor to sell me
I am sold out
have been
up and down
the river
and back.
Twhat?
There ain't no such place?
Then you will have to
meet me on the
printed page.
Where else
could we meet
but on the
printed page?
Say no ideas but in things.
But what is left
of a thing when
it is defaced
obliterated
its forms of love
alienated
from themselves
what is left then
but the idea of it?

What is left of the man-city
when the city is gutted out
beyond recognition
beyond remorse
where nothing but
abstractions remain
where things stood before.
(Name names! Name cities!
Beirut! Tehran! San Salvador!)
When blood itself is spilled
beyond measure
beyond accounting
the hot precious blood
what substance remains then
in what form of what love?
What island in what blood
when even islands
are set adrift
in an alien sea
in an alien element
that thins out the blood
that suffers not the fury
of the love which is the man?
Naked in this body of flesh
in this body of water
your nakedness your sole
arm and armor
in a savage sea
that suffers not your metal.
Crying out your words
in the face of the water
in the face of the wind
in a deadly discourse
with the elements

in which the sea
your prompter fills
your hollow words
with salt water.
This is a man's necessity now
his radiant gist
in the blessed year
of Our Lord 1982.
Say, No, if you can!
Say, 'Tain't so!
Say that to the Marines!
Say that to Robert Moses
who built cities and knew men.
"If the end doesn't justify
the mean, what does?" said he.
"Nothing I have ever done
has been tinged
with legality."
And they buried him big
like a true prophet
that he was.
Eulogized him to death.
Hurrah for Moses!
He was right on the money!
You about to begin
to get my drift, eh?
That was a bad joke
you played on me
Gloucester, root-city.
Here coming
all that way
across the ocean
to make your polis mine
or whatever is left of it

only to discover that
Moonies have bought you out.
The Fat Reverend owns you now
every blessed man in it
and every blessed fish
hooked.
News to you?
In-cor-porated.
Transsubstantiated
into the corporate body
of Christ? Hell, no!
Of course no one knew
they were sold out
until they were.
They never do.
Oh, the days when even names
were honest, were not "staged,"
were not something to hide behind
when a man died with
the name he was
born with, when
a Smith meant a Smith
a Brown meant a Brown.
Now they'll probably name it
Hooker Fishing Town, Inc.
Remember Hooker Chemical?
Was no one in Love Canal
smart enough to figure out
what they were all about
until it was too late?
They sure know how
to pick their names, though.
Would you buy a dream house
from a Hooker Company?

Sure as they knew then
how to pick their generals.
General George A. Custer!
General George Crook!
Would you buy a second-hand
treaty from a General Crook?
They did, Indians did
see through them though.
But there was
not a damn thing
they could do.
Nor is there
a damn thing
you could do
or I!
Yes, we will
put up a fight
as the salmon does
the brave salmon
the valiant salmon
who braves oceans
and waterfalls
to get back
to her roots
who shoots through
love's hell to
embrace a grave.
But Salmon
swims in a stream
not in this sewer
not in this
Love Canal.

II

No, I am not Aeneas!
Came not here to build Rome!
Could not carry
my father's corpse
on my frail shoulders.
I just ran from a city
from a burning city
from a burning hell
where the fire
like Hell's fire
did not consume
did not purify
the flesh it burned,
where I could not
kill kill kill,
where the choice was
to dig in or to pull out
to kill or to be killed.
I had always thought
my job as protecting
mankind against itself.
I was the mender
of bits and pieces
of broken humanity.
I used to walk
on the frozen river
where children skated on ice.
I walked close to the abutment
where water still flowed,
walking on eggshells.
When I was there

the children were safe.
I was their tester of the ice,
not for pay but for love.

Now here I sit
broken Adam in my weeded garden,
waiting to rename, to recreate,
contemplating my burning Troy,
my burning forms of love,
fishing in the river
of my blood for roots
I can concoct into
new love potions.

III

If old gods are not buried,
there will be no sap in the soil.
If new land is not plowed,
there will be no new seeding.
If new virgins are not
broken at new altars,
there will be no new blood,
there will be no new brides.
If there are no new brides
there will be no new virgins.

Bury your old dead
in the old land.
Leave your old graves
in the old valley,
where new floods
will wash them clean.

A new Adam rises
with the new sun,
renames, recreates,
mirrors himself,
in the virgin spring.
Unbends the frail shoulders,
spruces up, freshens
the old face.
Here's a new beginning
in a new land,
new loves to be made,
new hates to be harbored,
new hay to new market.